Linda —

Enjoy!

Stuff That Works
Every Single Day

Larry Winget

Also by
Larry Winget

The Ya Gotta's For Success!

The Little Red Book Of Stuff That Works!

Money Stuff — How to increase prosperity, attract riches, experience abundance and have more money!

101 Things That Make You Say UNGAWA!

Stuff That Works Every Single Day

Larry Winget
Copyright ©MCMXCIV

Printed in the United States of America.
Cover design by Ad Graphics, Tulsa, Oklahoma.
ISBN: 1-881342-03-4
Library of Congress Catalog Number: 94-090256

"Stuff That Works™" is a trademark of Win Publications!, Win Seminars!,
and Larry Winget, denoting a series of books and products including pocket
cards, calendars, audio cassettes and videotapes.

Published by:
Win Publications!
a subsidiary of Win Seminars!, Inc.
P. O. Box 700485
Tulsa, Oklahoma 74170
918 745-6606

Order information:
Call Toll Free:
800 749-4597

Dedication

To my wife Rose Mary and my boys, Tyler and Patrick.

January
1

Expect the best.

Be prepared for the worst.

Celebrate it all!

January

2

Prepare for the future.

You will spend most of your time there.

January
3

Life is not a restaurant;

they don't bring it to you.

Life is a buffet;

you have to serve yourself.

January
4

Focus on a belief system of loving and serving

others through your life, your words,

your products, and your service,

and success and prosperity will always be yours.

January
5

Continually ask yourself,
"What is the most valuable use of
my time right now?"

January
6

Never underestimate your ability

to accomplish the impossible.

January
7

Implement now.

Perfect later.

January
8

The most useless day of all is

that in which we have not laughed.

Sebastien Roch Nicolas Chamfort

January
9

You must see it first in your mind if you are ever going to see it in your reality.

January
10

What you think about

and talk about,

comes about.

January
11

You can always have just as much

success as you believe you deserve.

January
12

Prejudice is ignorance.

It is the result of not knowing and not understanding.

Prejudice is also based in a lack of self worth.

If we felt good about ourselves it wouldn't be

necessary to tear others down. We never lift

ourselves by tearing down someone else. We can

only lift ourselves by building others up.

January
13

If you lack any good thing,

you are still asleep to your own good.

Florence Scovel Shinn

January
14

Say Thank You often.

People want our appreciation more

than just about anything else.

January
15

Fill your mind with the pure,

the powerful, the positive, and the prosperous.

January
16

You don't have to be good to start,

but you do have to start to be good.

January
17

Life is an opportunity for you to

contribute love in your own way.

Bernie Siegel, M. D.

January
18

Think like a winner,

act like a winner,

and look like a winner.

People love to associate with winners!

January
19

After all is said and done,

more is said than done.

January
20

When you win at the expense

of someone else,

you do not win - you lose.

January
21

When it quits being fun - quit!

January
22

Love problems.

You will be compensated in

life in direct proportion to your

ability to solve problems.

January
23

People will pay you money to a great

extent based on what value

you place on yourself.

Jack Boland

January
24

People won't pay attention to what you have to say.

Most won't even believe what you have to say.

People will only pay attention to see if you

believe what you have to say.

January
25

When you miss the target,
never in history has it been
the target's fault.

January
26

Your best is always good enough.

January
27

Happily pay your bills and taxes.

Money will come to you exactly

as it goes from you.

January
28

Keep on succeeding,

for only successful people can help others.

Dr. Robert Schuller

January
29

When you are afraid of something,

you give it the power to hurt you.

January
30

Choose health. Never accept that sickness is natural. Refuse to be victimized by "the cold and flu season" and other popular negative beliefs that tell us we are supposed to be sick from time to time. Instead, daily affirm that you are healthy.

January
31

Your results have been determined

by your beliefs.

Change your beliefs and you will

change your results.

February
1

Whatever things are true, whatever things are noble, whatever things are just, whatever things are pure, whatever things are lovely, whatever things are of good report, if there is any virtue and if there is anything praiseworthy - meditate on these things.

Phillipians 4:8

February
2

Of all the people who will never leave you,

you are the only one.

Joe Charbonneau

February
3

Like it or not, you always get results.

February
4

Life is perfectly fair. Those who say it isn't, don't understand how it works. We get from life exactly what we are supposed to; no more, no less. We create everything that happens to us. There are no accidents. We have total responsibility for our lives. It is ours to create just the way we want.

February
5

If you want to have more money,

serve more people. It's that simple.

If you have lots of money it is for the

simple reason that you are serving lots of people.

Not much money, not much service.

February
6

Results are everything.

They don't ask how, they ask how many.

February
7

Time is the only thing that you can never

get any more of. Never waste it.

Never allow anyone else to waste it for you.

Become aware of how you use your time.

February
8

It is better to under-promise and over-perform than it is to over-promise and under-perform.

February
9

Being late is nothing short of disrespectful. It shows that you don't care about the other person enough to make the effort to be on time.

February
10

Keep away from people who try to belittle

your ambitions. Small people always do that,

but the really great make you feel that you, too,

can become great.

Mark Twain

February
11

F ood.

Enjoy every bite of it.

Just don't take so many bites.

February
12

Make a lot money, get a lot of great stuff, surround yourself with people who love you, do something that you absolutely love to do, then destroy your health with cigarettes, alcohol, too much food and inactivity. How stupid is that?

February
13

Spread love everywhere you go:

first of all in your own house. Give love to your children, to

your wife or husband, to a next door neighbor . . . Let no one

ever come to you without leaving better and happier. Be the

living expression of God's kindness; kindness in your face,

kindness in your eyes, kindness in your smile, kindness in

your warm greeting.

Mother Teresa

February
14

The best way to get your spouse to change
is for you to change. Change the way you
talk about them. Change the way you act
toward them. Change the way you treat them.
When you change, they will change.

February
15

Become more educated about what you want to become. If you want to be a doctor, study medicine. If you want to be a lawyer, study the law. If you want to become successful, study success. Want money? Study money. Want to be healthier? Study health. See how it works?

16

Never work.

When it feels like work

you are doing something wrong.

February

17

Never confuse your career with

who you are. What you do and who you are,

are two different things.

February
18

G o Big or Stay Home!

February
19

It is easier to pay taxes on the money you have,

than to pay no taxes on the money you don't have.

February
20

Love what you do and do what you love.

To spend your life any other way is a waste.

February
21

People do business with people they know, like, and trust. Be trustworthy, likeable and get known by as many people as possible.

February
22

Stop believing in competition.
Competition says that two parties bring exactly
the same service to the marketplace. That is
impossible. There is always a difference. Find
that difference and exploit it and you will never be
without plenty of business.

February
23

Children are not just little adults.

Never expect of a child what you would of an adult.

They think differently and act differently.

They must be treated differently.

February
24

Everything in life gets better when we get better.

Business gets better when we get better.

Husbands get better when wives get better.

Wives get better when husbands get better.

Children get better right after parents get better.

When we want things to be better,

then we must get better.

February
25

Be as courteous with members of your family
as you would be with a stranger you would
really like to impress.

February
26

Live your life as if you were

an exclamation point!

February
27

It is impossible to offer anyone

"constructive criticism."

"Constructive" means to build up

and "criticism" means to tear down.

It is impossible to do both at the same time.

February
28

While you are a product of your environment

in many ways, it should never be used as

an excuse for poor results.

Your environment, good or bad,

is only a motivator, never a limiter.

February
29

It is the achievement of worthwhile goals that will create the future that you want your present to become.

March
1

Mediocre leaders train their people

to be better employees.

Outstanding leaders train their employees

to be better people.

March
2

When two people always agree,
one of them is no longer necessary.

March
3

Want to know what to read in order to be more successful? It's easy. Go to store and see what the poor people read. Then don't read that. Romance novels won't teach you one thing about success. Instead, ask someone who is successful in an area you are interested in to suggest some books they have read. When they do, then buy the books and read them.

March
4

If we just do what we love, love what we do,

and express ourselves fully and freely, we are serving

others in accordance with our purpose. All that is left

is for us to open ourselves to receive.

Arnold Patent

March

5

People want your passion.

They can get your information

from any number of sources.

March
6

Your ability to solve the problems of

other people will determine your success as well

as the amount of money you make.

In order to make more money, all you have to do is solve

bigger problems. The bigger the problem you solve, the

bigger the paycheck you will take home.

March
7

Habit is the number one enemy of success.

We must change our habits of thought and action

if we are to experience a change in our results.

March
8

You usually get exactly what you expect.

Train yourself to expect the best.

March
9

The best thing you can do for the
poor is to not be one of them.

Reverend Ike

March
10

Our chief want is someone who will inspire

us to be what we know we could be.

Ralph Waldo Emerson

March
11

Learn from the animals.

They eat when they are hungry

and quit eating when they are full.

They rest when they are tired. They never worry.

They don't care about money, yet have plenty.

They live in the moment.

Good advice.

March
12

It is more important to do the right thing

than to do things right.

March
13

We create our own reality.
If our perception of reality is one of lack and
limitation, then our reality will be lack and
limitation. If we perceive the world to be a
wonderful, loving, exciting place, then that will be
the kind of world we live in.

March
14

The best way to keep from going crazy regarding the condition of your teenager's room is to shut the door.

March
15

It is better to be prepared for an opportunity

and not have one than to have an opportunity

and not be prepared.

Whitney Young

March
16

The word happiness comes from the
same root word as happenstance or happening.
In others words, what is going on around us,
or what is happening, will determine whether we
are happy or not. Don't let this be true for you.
Never let your happiness depend on anything
external. Happiness comes from within.

March
17

Success is being the best you can be in each area of your life without sacrificing your ability to be your best in each and every other area of your life.

March
18

Opportunity is everywhere.

Opportunity can be found in every single thing

that happens to us and around us. We only have to pay

attention and look for the opportunity. Sometimes

opportunity is thrust upon us. Only we see it as a problem.

It's at those times that opportunity is not knocking,

it's kicking down the door.

March
19

Look as successful as you can possibly afford to.

Your clothes, car, and office should all be monuments to your

success. People like to do business with winners.

Look like a winner.

March
20

It's not the money - it's the stuff!

March
21

The kingdom of Heaven is here and now.

Create Heaven right where you are by loving;

forgiving; serving; letting go of fear; enjoying;

and being thankful.

March
22

Forget luck. There is no such thing as luck.

Things happen to us because they are supposed to happen.

Everything that happens does so for a reason.

Search out that reason and learn from it.

March
23

When we get mad at someone and give
them a piece of our mind, what we have
really done is give them our peace of mind.
Is it really worth it?

March
24

Listening is practically a lost art.
Maybe it's because we all think that what we have
to say is so important that we don't hear what
anyone else has to say. It's not that we can't listen
or don't know how to listen, it's that we don't
choose to listen.

March
25

Peace in the world will only happen when we

become at peace within ourselves.

March
26

"Ask and you shall receive."

We would have more if we would ask for more.

We don't always get what we deserve or what we need, and

we certainly don't get what we gripe about. We do, however,

get what we ask for. When we ask and don't receive, it is

because we didn't ask in the right way, or didn't ask the right

person, or didn't ask often enough. Asking is how we get.

Ask a little, get a little. Ask a lot, get a lot.

March
27

Remember birthdays and anniversaries.

Celebrate these dates and do your best to make them special.

Build memories that will last.

March
28

Few people will turn to themselves to take responsibility for their results until they have exhausted all opportunities to blame someone else.

March
29

Hang in there. Don't give up.

But don't be stupid about it either.

There is a time to walk away and let it go.

As the saying goes,

"When you find yourself on a dead horse, get off!"

March
30

Our thoughts, actions, words, and relationships either move us closer to where we want to be or farther away from where we want to be. Nothing is neutral.

March
31

Hard work never made anyone rich.

It will make you tired, but it won't make you rich.

April
1

Lighten up!

April

2

Television leads us to believe that

life is a spectator sport.

Life is not about watching,

it is about being and doing.

April
3

I may not be the man I want to be;

I may not be the man I ought to be;

I may not be the man I could be;

I may not be the man I can be;

but praise God, I'm not the man I once was.

Martin Luther King, Jr.

April
4

Being a parent means that you are the mother or the father. It doesn't mean that you are always right. Sometimes you are wrong. Admit it. Say you're sorry.

April
5

We often hear that happiness is a choice.

It isn't. Unhappiness is a choice.

Happiness is our natural state of being.

April
6

You cannot be totally committed sometimes.

A Course In Miracles

April
7

Stuff doesn't cost too much.

You just don't have enough money.

Don't blame the stuff for something that is your fault.

April
8

Nature abhors a vacuum.

In order to have more of the good stuff in our lives,

we must make room for it. This means that we must

give away some of the stuff we have. When we give

away our stuff, we have created a vacuum and

Nature will spring into action to fill the void.

April
9

What is easy to do is also easy not to do.

Jim Rohn

April
10

Success, happiness, health, and prosperity

are yours by Divine Right and can never

be taken away from you!

April
11

When someone says,

"I want to tell you this for your own good,"

understand that it is really not for your own good.

It is for their own good. Refuse to be victimized

by this controlling behavior.

April
12

Worry is the abuse and misuse of the imagination.

It is negative visualization.

Don't waste your time picturing or thinking

about what you don't want to happen.

Instead, focus on what you really

do want to happen.

April
13

A guaranteed way to avoid criticism:

Say Nothing.

Be Nothing.

Do Nothing.

April
14

Any fact facing us is not as important

as our attitude toward it, for that

determines our success or failure.

Dr. Norman Vincent Peale

April
15

Good leaders never tolerate mediocrity.
Mediocrity hurts co-workers, the customer,
the leader and the employee.

April
16

Know your stuff. Believe in your stuff.

Don't take anyone else's stuff. Make sure that your stuff

works. Give some of your stuff away. Enjoy your stuff.

Don't become too attached to your stuff.

Be thankful for your stuff.

April
17

Success is predictable.

Simply repeat what successful people

have done and you will achieve similar results.

April
18

A good four letter word to remember: NEXT.
When something happens that you aren't pleased with,
just say "next." When something good happens, say
"next." The business of life is moving forward. Say
"next" and move on.

April
19

Don't bother trying to enlighten people who need your help. Those who need it rarely appreciate it. Instead, spend your time with those who want your help. When a person wants to be helped the exchange is much more rewarding for both parties.

April
20

Refuse to participate in any type of negative talk.

April
21

Spend some time every day in silence.

It doesn't really have to be very long,

just a few minutes at least twice a day.

April
22

Smile more often.

It will make you feel better about yourself

and other people will like you more.

April
23

Be as quick to point out good service

as you are to point out bad service.

April
24

The difference between honesty and integrity?

Honesty is telling the truth.

Integrity is feeling good about having done it.

April
25

Begin every day by writing down five

things you are thankful for.

This will help you maintain an attitude of

gratitude all day long.

April
26

Be an encourager.

Put courage into people with your words,

your support, and your love.

April
27

You will drive yourself crazy trying to figure out why
people do the things they do. Don't bother with it.
People do what they do because that's what they do.
You can't really do anything to change what people do
anyway, so accept people the way they are.

April
28

Success comes from what you do,

not from what you are going to do.

April
29

Be known as someone who gets it done fast.

April
30

For God's gift to you is more talent and ability, than you will ever use in one lifetime. Your gift to God is to develop and utilize as much of that talent and ability as you can in this lifetime.

Bob Proctor

May
1

When you believe you were born a winner,

then you will act with the confidence of a winner

and bring about winning results.

May
2

Speak in terms of your blessings

rather in terms of your challenges.

Catherine Ponder

May
3

Your words are the outpicturing of your

consciousness. If you want to know what you

really believe, listen to your words.

Nothing can change until your words change.

Jack Boland

May
4

Never say, "I can't afford it."

As long as you are saying what you can't afford,

you will never be able to afford it.

May
5

Whatever you vividly imagine, ardently desire,

sincerely believe, and enthusiastically act upon must

inevitably come to pass.

Paul J. Meyer

May
6

Hating what you do is a miserable way to live your life. Don't do it. Refuse to be unhappy. Choose to live a life of fulfillment. This can be done only by loving what you do and doing what you love.

May
7

No pain, no gain.

A stupid statement.

If you sincerely believe that you must experience

pain before you can reap the reward,

then get ready for the pain.

May
8

At the moment you discover any truth, even a small one, you are obligated to share it. Not to share it is to steal from those who could use the information and benefit from it. Not sharing it also robs you of the joy you will feel from sharing it. It will also block the flow of good into your life. To keep the good coming in, you must keep it flowing.

Give away what you know.

May
9

The truth does not need defending.

May
10

Love is the ultimate spiritual experience.

Love is the key to success and prosperity.

Love is the greatest of all gifts.

May
11

There is no future in saying, "I should have" or "I could have" or "I wish I had" or "If only."
You can't have a great future or even a great present when you are living in the mistakes of the past.

May
12

What we think determines what we believe;

what we believe influences what we choose;

what we choose defines what we are;

and what we are attracts what we have.

Jim Rohn

May
13

If you don't like who you are, change it.

If you aren't happy with what you have, change it.

If you don't enjoy what you are doing, then change it.

You have the ability to change any condition.

Your life never has to be same again after today.

May
14

This is the single greatest cause of difficulties and deterioration in relationships - the need to make the other person wrong, or to make yourself right.

Dr. Wayne Dyer

May
15

Anytime you do less that your best, you are stealing.

You are stealing from your employer,

your customer, your family, and yourself.

May
16

Money is the symbol of duty,

it is the sacrament of having done for mankind

that which mankind wanted.

Samuel Butler

May
17

We attract to us what we first become.

May
18

The Law of Cause and Effect doesn't play favorites.

It doesn't like one person more than another.

In fact, it doesn't like or dislike anyone.

The Law just is. Period.

You can make it work for you or you can

cause it to work against you.

It is your choice.

May
19

Your beliefs determine everything.

Your beliefs will determine every word you say and every

action you take. Your beliefs will determine your results, the

amount of money you have, the kind of car you drive, the

house you live in, and the quality of your relationships.

All are determined by your beliefs.

May
20

No amount of anything is enough.

Only your best is enough.

May
21

Keep your money circulating.

If you hoard it for a rainy day,

you may have to spend it on an ark.

John Randolph Price

May
22

You always have options.

May
23

We all learn only one way: spaced repetition.

Spaced repetition says that what goes into our mind

over and over again will become a part of us.

Stand guard at the door of your mind.

May
24

Never say something stupid like,

"Things can never get worse."

If there is one thing that things can always get,

it's worse.

May
25

You have to meet people where they are in order

to lead them where you want them to go.

May
26

Life is for you and me. It is ready

to give us whatever we claim;

whatever we aim for we will obtain.

Mark Victor Hansen

May
27

You'll know that you are really successful
at what you do when you can't tell the difference
between work and play.

May
28

It's not what happens to you that matters,

it's what you do about what happens

to you that matters.

May
29

Take ten deep breaths every morning.

This will clear your mind and oxygenate your blood system.

You will feel better and live longer.

May
30

Life is too short to nag your family and friends

about all of the little things.

Nag less, hug more.

May
31

Be the kind of person your dog thinks you are.

June
1

It is useless to affirm benefits, protection, supply, guidance, and healing, if all the time you are doing things which you know are not right in the sight of God and man.

Catherine Ponder

June
2

When you believe that life is for you and that you can be

prosperous and successful, then you will act that way and

end up with that as your result.

June
3

No one cares about what you do.

They only care about what you get done.

June

4

Love is the key to all success. Love for

what you do, love for the people you do

it for, love for your product or service,

and love for yourself.

June
5

Ask more. Listen more. Tell less.

June
6

No matter what area of your life you want to develop, there is a book that can teach you how to become successful in that area.

However, buying the book won't do you any good.

You have to read the book.

Then you have to take action on what you've read.

Only then does a book have any value.

June
7

The more you are thankful for what you have,

the more you will have to be thankful for.

Zig Ziglar

June

8

You have to be before you can do,

and you have to do before you can have.

June
9

Probably the hardest thing for us to do is take responsibility.
We have been conditioned to blame. We blame the economy,
our geographic location, our business, our boss, our spouse,
the weather, our environment, and so on. We blame
everything except the proper thing: ourselves. We all have
the same list of things to work with. One person can take the
list and become a millionaire. Another can take the very
same list and go broke. It's obviously not the list.
It must be something else; it must be us.

June
10

Your ability to get along with other people is one of the most valuable assets you possess.   Your effectiveness as a leader, salesperson, co-worker, parent, spouse, or anything else is dependent on your ability to effectively get along with others.

June
11

Life is an opportunity for you to

contribute love in your own way.

Bernie Siegel, M. D.

June
12

Give what you lack.

If you need money, give away some of the

money you now have. If you need more time, give

a little of your time to someone else. Anything

that you need will come to you when you give

away some of what you already have.

June
13

Ask, and it shall be given you; seek,
and you shall find; knock, and it shall
be opened unto you: for everyone that
asks receives, and he that seeks finds, and
to him that knocks it shall be opened.

Matthew 7: 7-8

June
14

You are a reflection of

what you see, what you hear,

and the people you associate with.

June
18

Suspend disbelief!

June
15

Smiles are reciprocal.

When you want one, give one away.

June
16

When we listen to someone we show them respect.
We aren't obligated to agree and we certainly don't need to
argue. We only need to listen. What someone says is
important to them. We need to show them how much we
care for them by listening to them.

June
17

Go to health food stores.
Do your best to stay healthy naturally
It is much better to stay healthy
than it is to get well after you have becom

June
19

Everything we have,

good or bad, is the result of some action we took.

June
20

Rejoice and be glad in the progression,

advancement, and prosperity of all men.

Whatever you claim as true for yourself,

claim it for all men everywhere.

Do not ever try to deprive another of any joy.

Joseph Murphy

June
21

If you really want to be rich,

do what you love and love what you do.

You will enjoy it more, be better at it,

and be paid more for it.

June
22

Love yourself.

When you love yourself you will take care of yourself

physically, mentally, and spiritually. You will expect the best

from yourself and do your best at all times.

June
23

Don't borrow books.

Other people don't want you to write or mark in their

books. Don't loan your books to anyone.

You will probably never get them back. Buy others their

own copy. It's a great way to show you care about them, a

great way to share the joy you received from a great book,

and a great way to hang on to your own books.

June
24

When faced with a mountain I will not quit!

I will keep on striving until I climb over;

find a pass through, tunnel underneath,

or simply stay and turn the mountain

into a gold mine with God's help!

The Possibility Thinker's Creed

Dr. Robert Schuller

June
25

Every experience is the result of a corresponding

cause that we put into effect by our thinking,

beliefs, actions, and words.

June
26

Catch your children doing something right.

Praise their specific behavior.

Good behavior, when rewarded,

gets repeated.

June
27

One of the keys to time management is
the effective use of the trash can.

June
28

Most people think they want more money

than they really do, and settle for a lot less

than they could get.

Earl Nightingale

June
29

There is no box made by God nor us

but that the sides can be flattened out and the top

blown off to make a dance floor on which to

celebrate life!

Kenneth Caraway

June
30

The good life is not ours for the taking,

but for the giving and accepting.

July
1

When faced with a dilemma:

Stick with it for all you are worth.

Give it your very best.

Explore every option possible.

Then give yourself permission to let

go and move on.

July

2

Conditions and circumstances

do not shape your destiny;

decisions shape your destiny.

July
3

Take care of yourself.

Exercise.

Eat right.

Don't smoke.

Don't drink too much.

"To be rich and sick is stupid."

Tom Hopkins

July

4

Give thanks for freedom.

Freedom to worship any way we choose.

To live any way we want to live. To be anything

we want to be. To have as much as we want to

have. To go anywhere we want to go. To say

anything we want to say.

What a country!

July
5

Take a moment right now to appreciate yourself. You are unique. No one is exactly like you. No one has your talent, your ability, your aptitude, or your potential. No one can contribute exactly what you have to contribute. You are a Divine creation.

Celebrate yourself!

July
6

The closer to the source, the purer the content.

This goes for food as well as information.

July
7

Never pity anyone their circumstances. Know that they created their own circumstances and must be there in order to learn. Instead, encourage them to think better of themselves and to see their unlimited potential. At that point, their circumstances will automatically improve.

July
8

First class is an attitude, not a seat on an airplane.

July
9

Only involve yourself in activities that you truly enjoy. If you don't want to go to the party, then don't go. If you don't want to be with a certain group of people, then don't be with those people. Life is too short to spend it doing things that we don't want to do.

July
10

Read great books.

No matter what area of life you want to
become better in, someone has written a book
in that area. You will be better off if you read
that book. Go to the bookstore. Buy the
book. Read the book.

July
11

Life is too short to be little.

Disraeli

July
12

Experience is the best teacher.

The problem with experience is that it takes too

long and costs too much. It is better to learn

from other people's experience.

July
13

Pay attention to a person's actions and not their
words. Some people have the words of a winner and
have the actions of a loser. These people are losers.
They are known as "articulate incompetents."

July
14

It is rarely personal.

July
15

Life really is black or white.

Everything is either right or wrong; good or bad.   You are

either on the way or in the way. It's hello or good-bye.

It either moves you closer to where you want to be

or farther away from where you want to be.

There is no gray.

July
16

Never compromise.

There is a way for everyone to win.

Take the time to discover that way.

July
17

Get your attitude right about money.

Money is a good thing.

You deserve all the money you need in order to

have the things you want.

There is enough money in the world for

everyone to have plenty.

Having plenty of money really can happen to you.

July
18

Success does not come from doing any extraordinary

thing. It comes from doing ordinary things,

extraordinarily well.

July
19

Spend your money willingly and freely. Not foolishly! Enjoy sharing the money you have. Of course you should save and invest some of your money. However, you should also learn to spend without fear. Don't think that poverty might be thrust upon you at any moment, so you had better put some away for a rainy day. You have never really spent the last of your money.   More money is always on the way.

July
20

Every day in every way I am growing more

prosperous, successful, victorious.

I am made for peace, health, and plenty, and I

am now experiencing them in ever-increasing

degrees in my life!

Catherine Ponder

July
21

Do more than you need to. Go farther than you need to.

Study more than you need to. Give more than you have to.

Always be your very best,

and then some.

"There are no traffic jams in the extra mile."

July
22

When a person makes five dollars an hour, they are probably solving five dollar problems and it take them about an hour to do it. When a person makes five thousand dollars an hour, they are probably solving five thousand dollar problems and taking about an hour to do it. When you want more money, learn to solve bigger problems, or learn to solve more problems of the same size in a shorter period of time.

July
23

You are only lonely when you don't like

the person you are alone with.

Dr. Wayne Dyer

July
24

Forgiveness in love is an absolute necessity for the

successful demonstration of prosperity.

Dr. James Melton

July
25

The worst thing that could happen, rarely happens. Stop picturing it. Stop expecting it. Start now to picture and expect what you do want to happen. Picture and expect only the best for yourself.

July
26

Look up the word "bless" in your dictionary.

You will find that one of the meanings of this little word is

"to confer prosperity upon." So start blessing. Bless

yourself. Bless your stuff. Bless your friends.

Bless your enemies. Bless your family.

Bless everything and everyone.

July
27

Ignorance stays with us until the day of
enlightenment, until our vision toward the
Spirit broadens and casts out the image of a no
longer useful littleness.

Ernest Holmes

July
28

Relax. Stop chasing the good life.

Know that you deserve health, wealth, success, and an

abundance of every good thing. You already have all of these

things. Simply slow down and accept them. Enjoy!

July
29

Build your life and your business on principles instead of specific techniques and skills. Techniques and skills are always tied to certain situations and situations can only be counted on to do one thing: change. Principles are timeless. They will work for anyone at anytime in any situation. Principles endure. Principles, grounded in love and service, will assure your success.

July
30

"As you sow, so shall you reap."

Sow a little, reap a little.

Sow a lot, reap a lot.

Not reaping?

Then get some sowing going!

July
31

Identify the main goal for your life.

Write it down. Keep it with you at all times.

Read it several times a day. Focus on how it would feel to

achieve the goal. Know what it would look like, what it

would sound like, what it would taste like, and what it would

smell like to achieve the goal. Involve all of your senses in

the achievement of your goal. When you do this, it will

happen. Guaranteed!

August
1

Find a need and fill it . . . find a hurt and heal it . . .

find a problem and solve it.

Dr. Robert Schuller

August
2

Good enough isn't

good enough.

August
3

Throw away your To-Do Lists.

Get a To-Get-Done List. To-Do focuses on activity.

To-Get-Done focuses on accomplishment.

Always focus on accomplishment rather than activity.

August
4

The weirder you are and the stranger you dress,

the better you have to be.

August
5

In business, good results cover up a multitude of sins.

August
6

Good can only happen to us as

we allow good to happen through us.

August
7

When you miss the target,

never in history has it been the target's fault.

Unknown

August
8

Make time for those you love to be with

and the things you love to do.

What else is time good for anyway?

August
9

You were created perfect and are still perfect. The imperfections you see are based on a limited understanding of your own good. These imperfections are not real and therefore mean nothing. Stop believing in them and they will cease to exist.

August
10

Here is a test to find whether your mission

on earth is finished: if you're alive, it isn't.

Richard Bach

August
11

Practice does not make perfect.

Practice only makes permanent.

Perfection comes through practicing perfectly.

August
12

Expecting the best, even with an element of
skepticism, is a much better way to live
compared to resigning yourself to the
mediocre.

August
13

In order to break a bad habit,

it must be replaced by a good habit.

It is impossible to quit anything.

You can't just stop doing something.

You can only replace one activity with another.

August
14

Ask for help when you need it.

Don't expect others to read your mind.

Most people are more than willing to offer their help

when they know there is a need.

August
15

Love all Serve all.

Sign above the kitchen.

Hard Rock Cafe

Washington, D.C.

August
16

We all have the same amount of time. You have the same amount of time as the average billionaire. It's not how much time you have, it's how you use the time you have.

August
17

Lack and limitation exist only in our minds.

They do not exist in the Universe.

The Universe is perfect and abundant.

August
18

Read the biographies of great men and women.
Learn from the lives of others. Duplicate the
principles and actions of a winner and your
chances of being a winner are assured.

August
19

Affluence, unboundedness, and abundance are
our natural state. We just need to restore the
memory of what we already know.

Dr. Deepak Chopra

August
20

Life is profoundly simple.

We are the ones who complicate it.

August
21

Money is the manifestation of your beliefs and actions. If you have it, then your thinking and actions are causing that to be. If you don't have it, then your thinking and your actions are causing that to be as well. Change your thinking, change your actions, and you'll change the amount of money you have.

August
22

While we cry out for justice, I don't really believe
that justice is what we want. I'm not convinced that
we really want to receive justice for our every action.

I think what we really want is grace.

August
23

There is nothing more frustrating than to find out that you are excellent at doing something that didn't need to be done at all.

August
24

Education is not permanent.

You must continually be educating yourself.

It is a never ending process of self development.

August
25

Style and money

have little to do with each other.

August
26

Get good at selling. Your success

depends on your ability to sell

yourself and your ideas.

August
27

He who laughs . . . lasts.

Tim Hansel

August
28

Knowledge is not power.

The implementation of knowledge is power.

August
29

Simplify. Simplify. Simplify.

August
30

Most problems with customers come from unfair expectations. We expect them to be nice, caring, fair, honest, and competent. In other words, we expect them to be just like us: perfect. That simply isn't fair. The customer can be only one thing: right.

August
31

Buy the best shoes that you can afford. They will last longer, look better longer, and your feet will feel better. And keep them shined. People notice your shoes more than you think. Unpolished, scuffed shoes can ruin an otherwise terrific outfit.

September
1

Once you know what you want,

know why you want it.

With a strong enough why you can endure any how.

September

2

Remember the Hole Principle:

When you find yourself in one, stop digging.

September
3

Make your home and your business a
sacred place where you only speak well of
yourself and others.

September
4

Study all different types of religions.
Go to lots of different churches. There is no one
church that is right for everyone. They all have their
good points and they all worship the same God.

September
5

If you aren't using it on a regular basis, then get rid of it. Give it away or have a garage sale, but never clutter up your life or your space with stuff that you are not using.

September
6

Take lots of pictures. Look back at
them often to remember and celebrate
the good times.

September
7

Don't put off until tomorrow what can

be enjoyed today.

Josh Billings

September

8

Teenagers need our love and understanding,

not our criticism. Criticism only frustrates both

parties and does nothing to

change the behavior.

September

9

Be mindful of your appearance.

While it is not fair or right, people will still

judge you first by the way you look.

September
10

The chief purpose of life is to serve.

In fact, all success comes from serving.

Our time, our talents, and our money only have

value when they are used to serve. Give freely of

these things and you will always be assured of

having plenty.

September
11

Educate yourself in life skills.

Learn how to set and achieve goals, manage your time, improve your self-esteem, get along with other people, and improve your attitude. That's the stuff that will make you successful. Technical skills and abilities are only a small portion of your success.

Life skills are the major portion.

September
12

Give, and it will be given to you; good measure,

pressed down, shaken together, running over,

will be put into your lap. For the measure you

give will be the measure you get back.

Luke 6:38

September
13

Look for the good in people and in situations.

When you take the time to look for the good,

you will always find it.

September
14

Don't bother fixing the blame.

Instead, fix the problem.

September
15

Be more child-like.

Play more. Laugh more. Run more. Buy a toy.

Sit on the floor. Ask more questions. Go to the

zoo. Eat an ice cream cone. Nurture the

innocent, fun-loving child that is within you.

September
16

Perhaps puppy dogs never have back pains because they are always wagging their tails.

Gerald G. Jampolsky, M.D.

September
17

Should have, would have, could have, and

might have, are a total waste of your time.

They focus on the past. There is no future in

the past. Move on - focus on what will be.

September
18

When faced with a decision, ask yourself, "What

is the very worst thing that could possibly

happen?" Then relax, because it probably won't

happen. Just make the decision. Even if you find

out that you are wrong, you will know quicker.

September
19

The Three Reasons Every Person Should Go To

Work Every Single Day

1. To keep existing customers

2. To create new customers

3. To make ourselves and our organization the

   kind that other people want to do business with

September
20

Life rarely asks you to do whatever it takes. However, life will always ask you to be willing to do whatever it takes. Willingness is the key. If you have a list of 50 things that must be done in order to get what you want, and you aren't willing to do number 50, then don't bother starting on number 1. Before you know it, there will number 50 staring you in the face and everything done up until then will have been a waste of your time.

September
21

The average American will spend a total of 19,000 hours in their car. Don't waste it by listening to the radio. Make your car an institution of higher learning. Listen to the audio tapes of great speakers and of great books. Turn your windshield time into learning time.

September
22

Everything that happens is a good thing. It may be a painful thing, but it's still a good thing. You may have learned a lesson, taken an action, or become a better person as the result. Anytime you learn, take action, or become more, that's good!

September
23

Do what you love. Do what makes your heart sing, and never do it for the money. Seek ye first the kingdom of Heaven, and the Masaratti will get here when it's supposed to.

Marianne Williamson

September
24

The Real Key To Visualization

The most important thing to visualize is your
contribution to others. Without the contribution,
there is no reward. Visualize yourself performing the
service that will ultimately be rewarded with success
and prosperity. See yourself performing a service that
you love and see others benefiting from that service.

September
25

You can have everything in life you want if you will

just help enough other people get what they want.

Zig Ziglar

September
26

Make sure that the first thought you have at the

moment you wake up is a positive thought.

These first moments of the day will set the mood

for the rest of the day.

September
27

The Greatest Management Principle In The World:

What gets rewarded, gets done.

Michael LeBoeuf

September
28

Stop using the word, try.

When someone tells you that they will try to do

something, do you really believe that it will get done? I

don't think so. Either do it or don't do it. To try is to

warn yourself and others that it probably won't get done.

September
29

We have only three basic needs:

to belong, to be appreciated, and to be loved unconditionally.

To belong, we must include.

To be appreciated, we must first appreciate.

To be loved unconditionally, we must love unconditionally.

Pamela S. Carter

September
30

You can always have more,

because you can always do more and be more.

October
1

Attitudes are contagious. Bad attitudes are more contagious than good attitudes. That's just the way it works. Bad news travels faster than good news. Disease spreads quicker than health. Ignorance is more contagious than intelligence. Ask yourself the question, "Is my attitude worth catching?"

October
2

There is no failure in doing.
There is only failure in not doing. Even if you
don't do it as well as you could do it, or as well as
you wanted to do it, or as well as you will do it,
the bottom line is, you still did it! Celebrate the
success of doing it!

October
3

Take action now! Movement toward your goals will create momentum. The more you do, the more you will be able to do.

October

4

Keep company with people who lift you up

and cause you to be your best.

October

5

Believe.

Believe in your country. Believe in others. Believe
in what you do. Believe in what is good, just, and
right. Believe in the future. Believe in yourself.
Believe in something bigger than yourself.

October

6

Three words that will guarantee failure:

Could - Should - Won't.

Jim Rohn

October
7

Give advice sparingly.

Give love freely.

Give your time carefully.

Give yourself wholeheartedly.

October
8

Do more than you are paid to do and
you will eventually be paid more for what you do.

October
9

Make no little plans; they have no magic to

stir men's blood and probably themselves

will not be realized. Make big plans; aim

high in hope and work, remembering that a noble,

logical diagram once recorded will not die.

Daniel H. Burnham

October
10

The greatest plan in the world

won't work if you won't.

October
11

People who aren't fired with enthusiasm,

should be fired with enthusiasm.

Malcolm Forbes

October
12

Tell me thy company and
I will tell thee what thou art.

Cervantes

October
13

Use things and love people.

Not the reverse.

October
14

"If you are going to change your life, you need to start

immediately and you need to do it flamboyantly."

William James

Find something you can do today that will get you started

toward achieving your goals. Even if it seems very small.

Don't put it off. Take action now.

Do something today!

October
15

Never go to sleep immediately after watching the nightly news. Instead, go to sleep after filling your mind with positive, thankful thoughts. This will assure a pleasant night's sleep and you will awake much more rested and in a better frame of mind.

October
16

Be interested. Be interesting.

The more interested you are,

the more interesting you will be.

October
17

What you resist, persists.

Larry James

October
18

You never make yourself more right by

making someone else wrong.

October
19

The old saying, "I'll meet them half-way" won't work. What happens when the other person doesn't go their half of the way? Then the relationship never comes together. Successful relationships require that both people go the entire way.

October
20

Become a Reverse Paranoid.

Believe that the whole world is out there

plotting to do you good!

October
21

To turn the other cheek means to look at things one way, then turn and look at them another way. Everything can and should be looked at from more than one point of view.

October
22

If you want something you have never
had, you've got to do something you
have never done.

Mike Murdock

October
23

Pretend that everyone you meet is wearing a button that says, "Make me feel important!" Then do your best to really make them feel important.

October
24

Remember one of the most used phrases in the Bible:

"And it came to pass . . . "

It didn't come to stay! It came to pass!

October
25

And let us not grow weary while doing good,

for in due season we shall reap if we do not lose heart.

Galations 6:9

October

26

Guilt serves no purpose.

There is no way to go back and change anything.

So forgive yourself and move on.

October
27

Take your job seriously,

not yourself.

October
28

Everything matters;

both the little things and the big things.

Never make the mistake of saying "it's no big deal, it

can't make that much difference." That's just not true. It

all makes a difference - every thought; every idea; every

word; every conversation; every action; every letter;

every phone call; and every relationship.

October
29

Become a master-asker.

Ask more from your customers. Ask more from

your employer. Ask more from your employees.

Ask more from your family. But before you ask

more from anyone else, ask more from yourself.

October
30

Do as much as you can. Save as much as you can. Read as

much as you can. Play as much as you can.

Give as much as you can.

"Everything in excess, nothing in moderation.

Moderation is for monks."

Lazurus Long

October
31

On with the dance - let joy be unconfined!

Mark Twain

November

1

This Day

This day, I thankfully accept all of the good things that are coming my way. This day is full of excitement, love, energy, health, and prosperity. This day, people are calling on me to be of service to them and I respond by giving my very best. This day, I think and practice health in my life, refusing to accept anything less than perfect health. This day, I accept the abundance and prosperity that is mine and lovingly share it with others. This day, I focus on the moment and give no thought to the past or to the future. This day, I spend in total enjoyment of what I do. This day, I fill with loving thoughts and actions toward myself and all other people. This day, I spend in grateful appreciation of all that is mine. This day, this hour, this minute, this moment is all that I have and I will use it in celebration!

November
2

If you want to know what a person is really like, then observe them under pressure. Whatever is inside will come out when the pressure is on. Observe yourself as well. If you get angry when things don't go your way, it is because you have anger in you. If you respond to adversity with love or with laughter, it is because those things are within you.

November

3

Smile.

Smile whether you feel like it or not. People like to do business with people who are friendly. A smile makes you feel better and it will make the other person feel better. It will disarm tense situations better than most any other tool. It will make you more attractive, successful, and prosperous.

November
4

When you get a new piece of information, use it immediately! Don't wait to get a hundred good ideas before beginning. Don't wait for ten ideas or even two. Every good idea should be implemented as soon as you receive it. Sometimes it only takes one good idea to make a drastic difference in your life and your income.

November
5

Money is a by-product of your thoughts, beliefs, words, and actions. Money is a natural occurrence in the life of someone who lives purposefully in a spirit of love, service, and giving.

November

6

Live long and prosper.

The Vulcan Creed.

November
7

When you have finished your day, be done with it. Never save any of your load to carry on the morrow. You have done your best, and if some blunders and errors have crept in, forget them. Live this day, and every day, as if it all may end at the sunset, and when your head hits the pillow, rest, knowing that you have done your best.

Og Mandino

November

8

Never become so set in your ways that you get stuck.

November
9

Be on time.

Start on time.

Stop on time.

November
10

Regarding doing business with friends,

remember the best way to avoid conflict:

Friends Pay Full Price.

November
11

The best way to determine whether you

should do something is to look at the consequences

of not doing it.

No consequences? Skip it.

Big consequences? Do it.

November
12

Read odd stuff. Visit odd places.

Make odd friends. Hire odd people.

Cultivate odd hobbies. Work with odd partners.

Tom Peters

November
13

People want two things from any relationship. First, they want to know what is expected from them. Second, they want to know what they can expect from you. Clearly communicate both in advance in order to build more satisfying relationships personally and professionally.

November
14

Tips for being enthusiastic:

Start every day by thinking enthusiastically. The way you begin your morning will set the mood for your entire day.

Surround yourself with enthusiastic people. Enthusiasm is contagious. Catch it from others.

Give your enthusiasm away. The more enthusiasm you give away, the more you will have.

November
15

I believe that imagination is stronger than knowledge,

that myth is more potent than history.

I believe that dreams are more powerful than facts,

that hope always triumphs over experience,

that laughter is the only cure for grief.

And I believe that love is stronger than death.

Robert Fulghum

November
16

Discover the gift within you

and then know that it is your responsibility

to share that gift with others.

November
17

You will be able to manifest any good that you
desire once you believe that you can have it and
take action on that belief.

November
18

An idea plus a strong belief, combined with
energy and enthusiasm, and implemented with love will
always bring success and prosperity.

November
19

When we become lax in the expression of gratitude

we become little people with little minds, leading

little inconsequential lives.

Eric Butterworth

November
20

Walk away from people and situations

that keep you from being your best.

November
21

Regardless of the question, love is the answer.

November
22

We were not put here to make our living,

but to live our making; and by living our making,

to make our living.

Les Brown

November

23

Different is good.

November
24

Don't wait on someone else to show up

and fix your problems. They might not show up.

Your problems are your responsibility.

The answers all lie within yourself.

November
25

People don't come into your place of business

so that you can get anything.

They're sent so that you can give them love.

Marianne Williamson

November
26

There is no difficulty that enough love will not conquer. There is no disease that enough love will not heal. No door that enough love will not open. No gulf that enough love will not bridge. No wall that enough love will not throw down. And no sin that enough love will not redeem. It makes no difference how deeply seated may be the trouble. How hopeless the outlook. How muddled the tangle. How great the mistake. A sufficient realization of love will dissolve it all. And if you could love enough you would be the happiest and most powerful person in the world.

Emmet Fox

November
27

Theories are a waste of time until they are put to use.

Only then will change occur.

November
28

It doesn't take any money to make things

better for you or for the world.

It only takes the willingness to love.

November
29

It takes more than education,

more than hard work,

more than a positive attitude,

and more than perseverance to be successful.

It takes believing in your right to be successful

accepting your success,

and positive action.

November
30

What you say about others says

more about you than it does about them.

December
1

Never criticize yourself.

There are plenty of other people to do that for you;

like your friends, co-workers, and family.

December
2

Be open to your intuition.

Follow where you are led.

The path is always there.

Trust.

December
3

Daily we must train our thoughts to see only what
we wish to experience; and since we are growing into
what we are mentally dwelling upon, we should put
all small and insignificant thoughts and ideals out of
our thinking and see things in a larger way.

Ernest Holmes

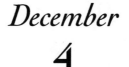

December
4

True happiness comes when what we do is in
alignment with our belief system and core values.

December

5

People and circumstances do not change because of

our criticism of what is wrong with them, but through

our support of what is right with them.

December
6

Putting another down for any reason is only putting
yourself down as we are all connected to each other and
interdependent on each other.

December
7

Stop identifying with your race, your gender, your age, your political affiliation, or your religious organization. Identify only with the Universal commonality that each of us shares with every other creation. Then celebrate the uniqueness with which the commonality is expressed.

December
8

Everyone that you come in contact with

is there to teach you something. Pay attention.

Become a willing student.

December
9

You are whole, complete,

and your success in life will be in

direct proportion to your ability to accept

this truth about you.

Dr. Robert Anthony

December
10

All work is a process.

When the process is based in love and service,

carried out with honesty and integrity, and

delivered with excellence and passion, then

outstanding results are automatic.

December

11

You will forgive others to the same extent that you forgive yourself.

December
12

Money is not success,

but success does include at least **some** money.

December
13

Let us not look back in anger or forward in fear,

but around in awareness.

James Thurber

December
14

The only thing constant is change.

Get good at dealing with change.

It is always going to be with us so it is useless to resist it.

Work with it instead of against it.

Use it to grow.

December
15

It is ridiculous to speak success and expect failure.
Your expectations of failure will cancel out your words
of success. When you are able to get your expectations
in alignment with your words, without any doubt or
fear, then your chances of success are assured.

December
16

Love is not an emptiness longing to be filled -

it is a fullness pressing to be released.

J. Kennedy Shultz

December
17

Humor that puts another person down just isn't funny. No joke should ever be made at the expense of someone else. Humor must be used carefully. The purpose of humor is to lighten another's load.

December
18

Doubt is a killer.

It will kill your chances for success, money, happiness, and good relationships. Doubt serves no purpose. Doubt never moves you forward, only backwards. More often, it will freeze you to a standstill. In order to achieve anything good in this life, you must say "no" to doubt. You must remember the power in the words, "It can happen!" And it really can, when you believe it and act upon it.

December
19

We find our happiness not in solving all the problems of the world, but in ceasing to be one of those problems.

J. Kennedy Shultz

December
20

People are always blaming their circumstances for what they are. I don't believe in circumstances. The people who get on in this world are the people who get up and look for the circumstances they want, and, if they can't find them, make them.

George Bernard Shaw

December
21

There is no way to happiness.

Happiness is the way.

December
22

Only
peace, kindness, harmony, balance, and love will bring
about success, prosperity, health, and happiness.

December
23

If any process or principle works at all,

then it works for all.

December
24

Affirmation without implementation

is self-delusion.

December
25

Decide to do what is right instead of what is popular.

When what is right becomes popular,

you will have achieved success.

December
26

The biggest problem our society faces is not poverty, homelessness, violence, drugs, promiscuity, disease, the deterioration of the family, or education. The biggest problem is a lack of love expressed for ourselves and other people. When we conquer this one, the others will cease to exist.

December
27

What you have done to create where you are,

can be undone to create where you want to be.

December
28

Stop hating the bad and start loving the good.

December
29

Good things come to us so they can be used by us in loving and intelligent ways.

December
30

Ask for exactly what you want in all situations.

Be very specific. This will improve your

relationships both personally and professionally.

December
31

God is not willing for you to
settle for anything less than everything.

Jack Boland

Larry Winget

Larry Winget knows what he's talking about! He has extensive experience in both the large and small business environments. He worked with AT&T and Southwestern Bell for over a decade and has owned three of his own businesses. He has experienced both incredible business success as well as total business failure. However, Larry is proof that you can go belly-up in business without going face-down in failure!

Larry now travels the country delivering speeches and seminars in the areas of Success, Prosperity, Sales, Leadership, Teambuilding, and Being Customer Focused. He is a member of the National

Speakers Association, a charter member and past president of the Oklahoma Speakers Association, and the founder of Win Seminars!

Larry is an author, speaker, consultant, trainer and entrepreneur. His unique combination of simple, straightforward, high-impact principles combined with humor and enthusiasm make his material fresh, fun and easy to apply.

His stories of his friend Cowboy, his dogs Elvis and Nixon, and Tarzan, Superman, and The Lone Ranger are classics that will make you laugh, cry and inspire you to succeed and keep life in the right perspective!

For more information on Larry's many books, tapes, speeches or seminars contact:

Win Seminars!
P. O. Box 700485
Tulsa, Oklahoma 74170
800 749-4597